Children Say the Funniest Things

A wonderful collection of hilarious little anecdotes and beautiful photos

SHELLEY COSTELLO

ISBN: 9781720050636

DEDICATION

For Whitney & Joel, the funniest, most beautiful two beings in the whole of the land and truly who inspired the book and much of its content.

INTRODUCTION

I don't know about you, but my children have me laughing out loud on a daily basis at the things they come out with. Every time I mention one of these funny little anecdotes or stories to a friend, they come back to me with something their own child has said, and the laughter continues.

It's no secret that laughter is the best medicine. We can learn a lot from our children, who on average by the way, laugh at least 300 times every day, compared to an average adult who is reported to laugh only 15 times a day!

I have been compiling these quotes since 2010 and the file has been opened and closed several times since. Fast forward 8 years and I have leapt into the unknown and following a love for photography. Over the years, I have taken hundreds of photos of families and a myriad of little people within and around them. After making the decision recently to publish a book of photographs, it occurred to me what a perfect unison the quotes and the photographs would make.

My motivation for publishing the book now, remains the same as back then; quite simply to make you laugh, warm your heart and leave you feeling good. Pick the book up, read a few pages, keep it in your bag, on your desk or somewhere handy and when you are feeling a bit down, under the weather or just have 5 minutes to spare, pick it up and laugh, smile and feel some emotion…. children live in the moment and truly do say the funniest things.

Thank you to everyone who contributed to compiling the quotes in this book. Without you it would not have been possible. Huge thanks to all the beautiful children who feature in the photographs - it makes my soul sing to look at these photos. Most of all thank you to my children, Whitney and Joel who are literally my purpose in life and make me laugh out loud every single day.

Finally, and most importantly, in keeping with the theme of children and contributing; all profits from the sale of this book will be donated to the NSPCC (National Society for the Prevention of Cruelty to Children). One of the most beautiful things about children (aside from the fact they are totally oblivious to how funny the things they say are) is that they live in joy in the moment. The NSPCC help give children their moments of joy back and for that reason it makes my heart swell to know that we are contributing in a small way to making that happen.

Thank you so much!

EnJOY,

Shelley Costello
Autumn 2018

"When I am 79, I will be able to walk to school by myself," Lola said.

My son was playing in the new tent and his sister was eating a lollipop. She got into a terrible mess, so I stripped her off and sent her back out to play.
My son came running into the house.
"Please don't let Summer in the tent," he yelled, "she'll set it on fire!"
"Don't be silly," I replied.
"She will," he continued, "there is a label in the tent saying, if you go in there naked, you'll start a fire!"

He had read the 'no naked flame' label…

When asked why his new dog was not home, Kirk replied,
"we took her to the vegetarian and had her sprayed."

He of course meant spayed by the veterinarian!

My daughter, Talitha, was always boisterous and wilful.
Trying to get her in the car seat each day was a challenge and she would arch her back to stop me putting on the straps.

"Please Tali, I need to do this, so I can drive home. You have to be strapped in for safety," I pleaded.
"Oh yes," she said, "well you get in the car seat then and I'll drive!"

Elizabeth came home from school one day with some funky looking cupcakes.
Full of pride she announced, “we made them out of scratch.”

"They didn't have toilet paper in the 80's," Lauren said,
"they had to use baby wipes."

While sitting with my nephew reading my daily, 'Message from God', on Facebook, he suddenly said,
"can you ask Jesus if he has holes in his hands please."

Helping my son with his homework project…

"Let's do a trifold leaflet," I said starting to fold the paper.
"Do you know what that is?" I asked him.

He thought for a moment…

"Yes, of course, it's where you try and fold it!"

My daughter came home from school one day and exclaimed, "my poo was really hard today, I think it was meant to come out tomorrow!"

My children were discussing food.

"I like sausages the most," Amy said.
"Well I like tuna," Jack responded and then said,
"but Mummy can't have those because she's a vegetable, aren't you Mummy?"

He actually meant vegetarian!

Lucy was chosen for the school cross country team.

"It's going to be great mum," she said,
"I've got to run a thousand centimetres."

My children started reading cereal boxes or sauce bottles on the table at meal times. They were enjoying hot dogs with ketchup one lunchtime…

"I can't believe it!" Josh said,
"This sauce was made in 1869!"

He was of course referring to the sauce company's established since date!

Pointing to the wooden chair, my son, Logan, exclaimed,
"Mummy, there's a splinter in the chair!"

We called Mateo several times to come down for dinner. When he finally came, we asked him why it had taken him so long.
He said,
“My leg fell asleep and it took me 10 minutes to wake it up!”

One morning my son, Ben, looked at our weekend in Norfolk photos.
I told him we were going back in the Easter holidays and we could hire a beach hut.
"Well I think that's a bit small for us all," he said,
thinking we were going to stay in it!

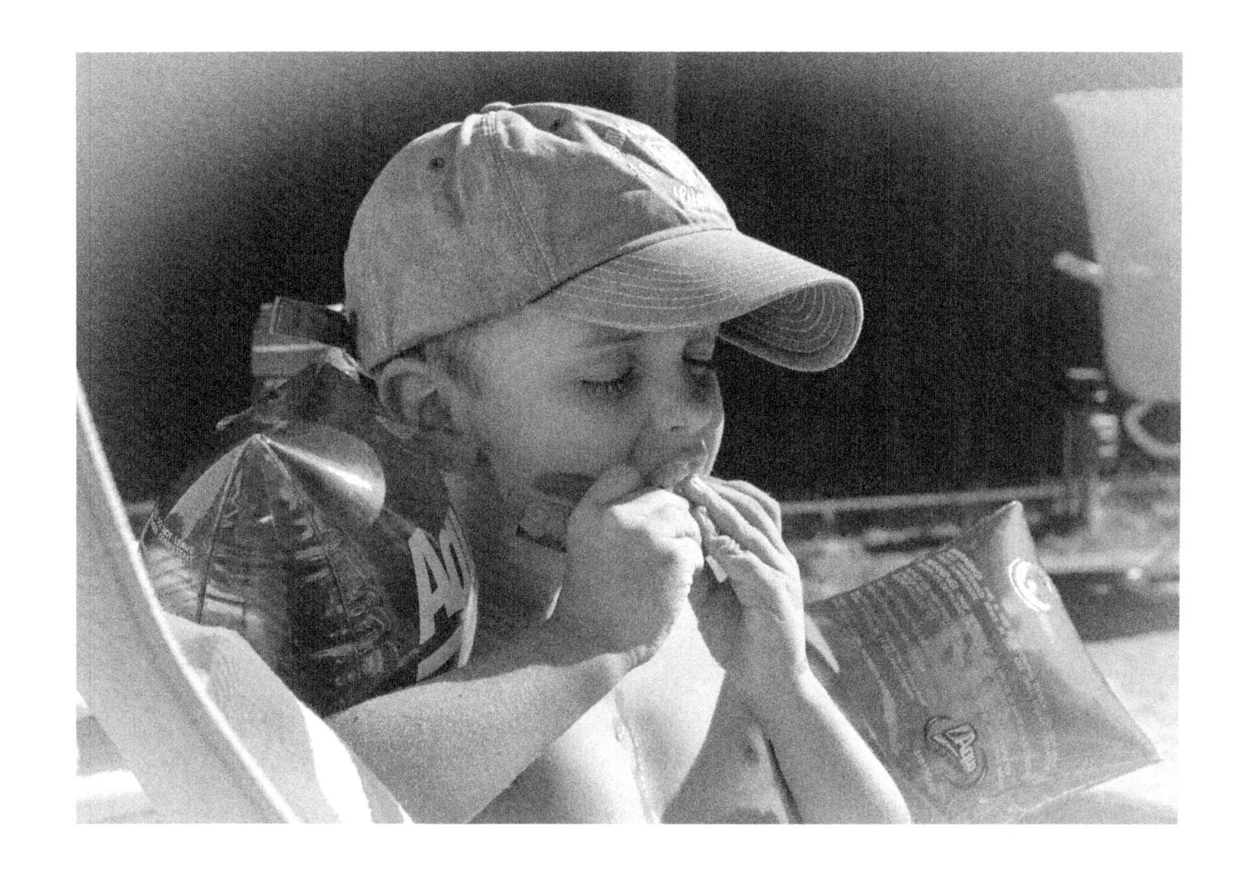

Joel was discussing school lunch with Whitney.
"We have to pay for ketchup," Whitney said.
"Well I go to a Christian school, so ketchup is free," Joel replied.

My daughter Chrissy, when seeing her first open top bus, exclaimed, "Look! That bus hasn't got a lid on it!"

I took some money out of the cash machine on the way to school one day.

"Wow you have £10 mum, that's a lot of money," my son said.
"I actually have £20," I said putting the two £10 notes into my purse.
"No, you definitely have ten," he replied, "because twenties are purple."

I was driving home one night in the fog with my two children,
Emily and Zac.
Emily and I were talking about the different times when we had been driving and it had been really foggy.
Then Zac said,
"did you know that the posh word for foggy is misty."

Mummy, did you know that in the olden days chefs were baddies?"
Skye asked me one day.
"Were they?" I asked, "are you sure?"
"Yes, because Robin Hood, the chef, was a baddie."

She actually meant the sheriff!"

Whitney asked if I had been playing on the Nintendo Wii.
"Don't be silly," Joel said,
"Mum doesn't play on the Wii because she's a 'yogable'."

I practice yoga and he was thinking along the lines of flexible.

"Do we have any hoss cross buns?" Charlotte asked.

Abbie was chatting to me one morning about the soap, Emmerdale.

"Mum, you know that woman in Emmerdale, the one who was with that man, Cain?" she asked.
"You mean Charity," I replied.
"Oh, yes, Charity," she said.
"I thought her name was Insurance," she said matter-of-factly.

She seriously thought that charity and insurance meant the same thing.

My son was talking to me about eating meat.

"You can't eat meat can you Mummy, being a 'verytarian'?" (his interpretation of the word vegetarian) he asked.
"Well I can, but I choose not to," I replied.
"That's ok anyway, Mummy, because you can eat 'verytarian' meat."

Herbie was doing his literacy homework and kept writing the words wrong.

"It's ok," I said, "you are just tired."
"I'm not tired," he replied, "I'm just confused."

"God would be really lucky if he was Santa," Joel said.

My daughter was messing about with my husband and pulled his eyelids up
so she could only see the whites of his eyes.
"Daddy?" she asked looking worried, "where have you gone?"

"We are going to Miami," I told my daughter.
She ran to tell her sister.
"We are going to Miami!" she exclaimed.
"No, we are not! We are not going to your ami," she said,
and then pointed at me,
"we are going to her ami."

My nephew was helping me prepare dinner.

As I was chopping lettuce he asked,
"where does lettuce come from?"
"It grows out of the ground," I replied, continuing to chop.
"That's right, it grows on a lettuce tree," he said pleased with himself.

I'd been explaining the law of attraction to my daughter. I said, that if you focus on something hard enough, you can bring it into your life and make it happen, just by thinking about it.

She was silent for a couple of minutes and I turned to see she was staring intently out of the window, which was open half way.
I carried on driving and felt a little chilly, so pressed the window button to put the window back up.

She jumped out of her skin, "oh my God!" she cried, "it works mum, it actually works! I was just sitting here staring at the window telling it to shut with my mind, you know like you said about focusing hard and making it happen. I made the window shut with my mind!" she exclaimed.

We laughed all the way home when I told her I had shut the window.

I was sitting outside in the sunshine with my two children when my daughter randomly said,

"Mummy, if you eat a snail, then you can eat everything."

My daughter was getting ready for school and said she hoped her teacher was going to be there because she had been poorly recently…

…with asthma fever apparently.

"How many people has God actually made?" my daughter asked.

ABOUT THE AUTHOR

Shelley Costello is a passionate writer, photographer and devoted practitioner of Ashtanga Yoga. She has published two previous books and a myriad of articles around wellbeing and yoga. She lives in England with her two, not so little anymore, children.

You can connect with Shelley on her photography site at www.shelleycostello.co.uk and her blog www.maldivesforthemind.com

Printed in Great Britain
by Amazon

26979188R00044